MY FIRST
LETTER AND NUMBER
TRACING BOOK

This Book Belongs To

....

....

Trace The Alphabets

Apple

Ball

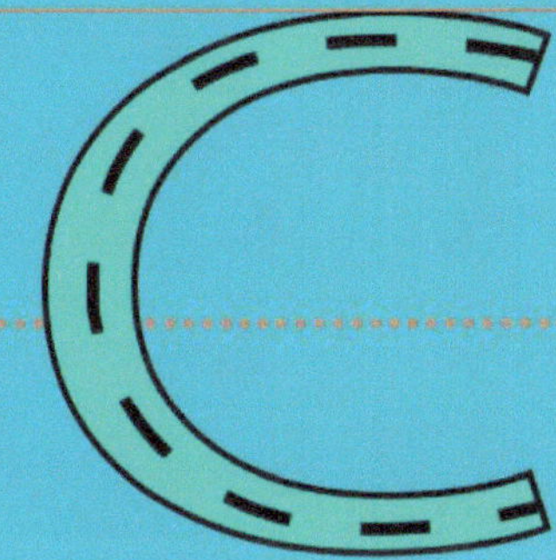

Cat

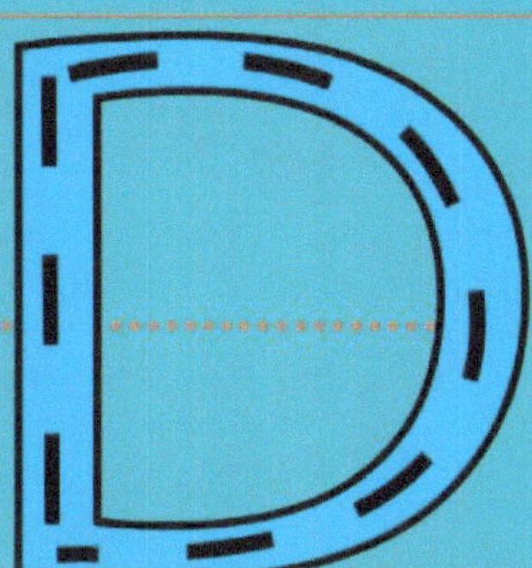

Dog

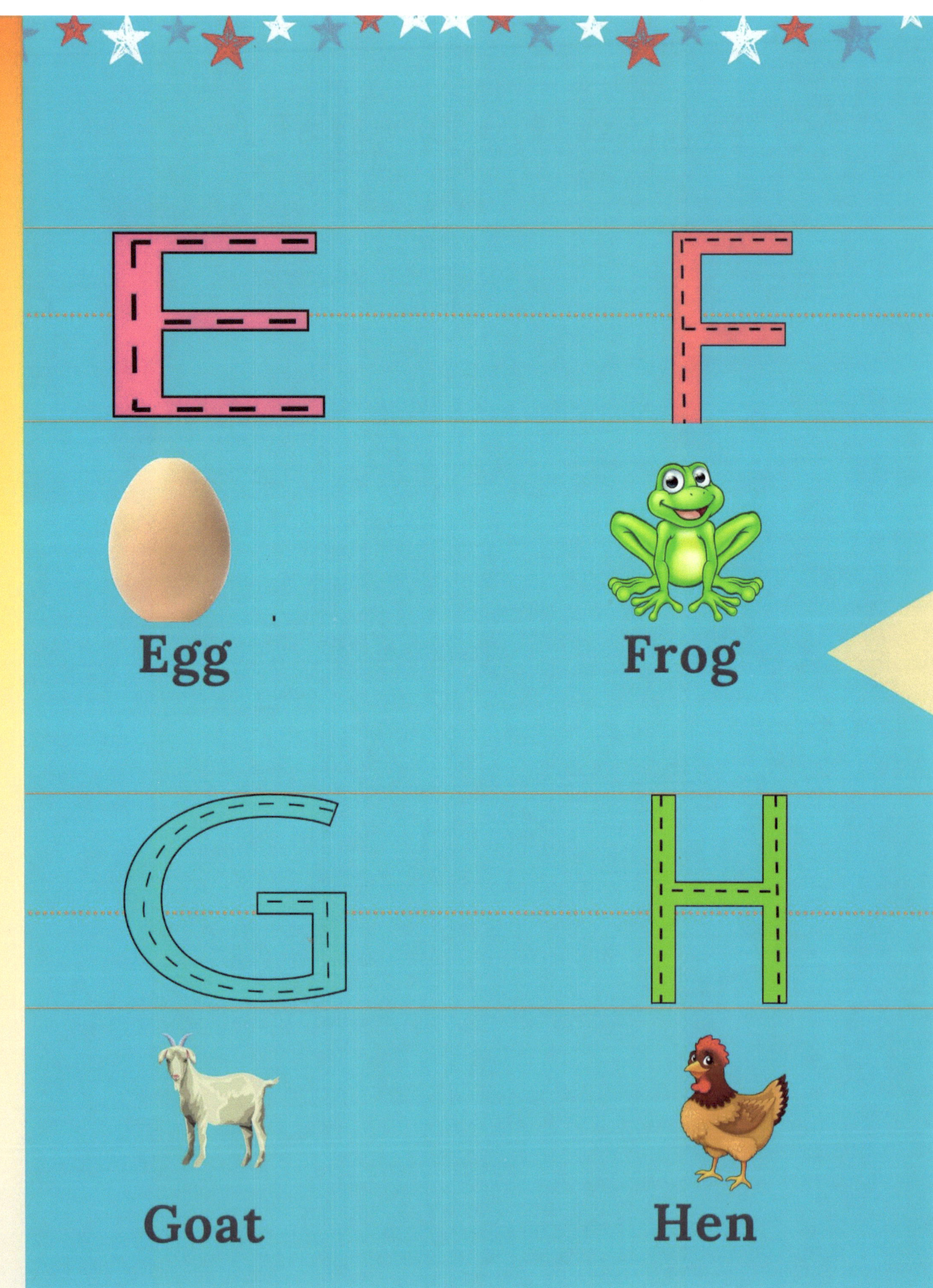
E
F
Egg
Frog
G
H
Goat
Hen

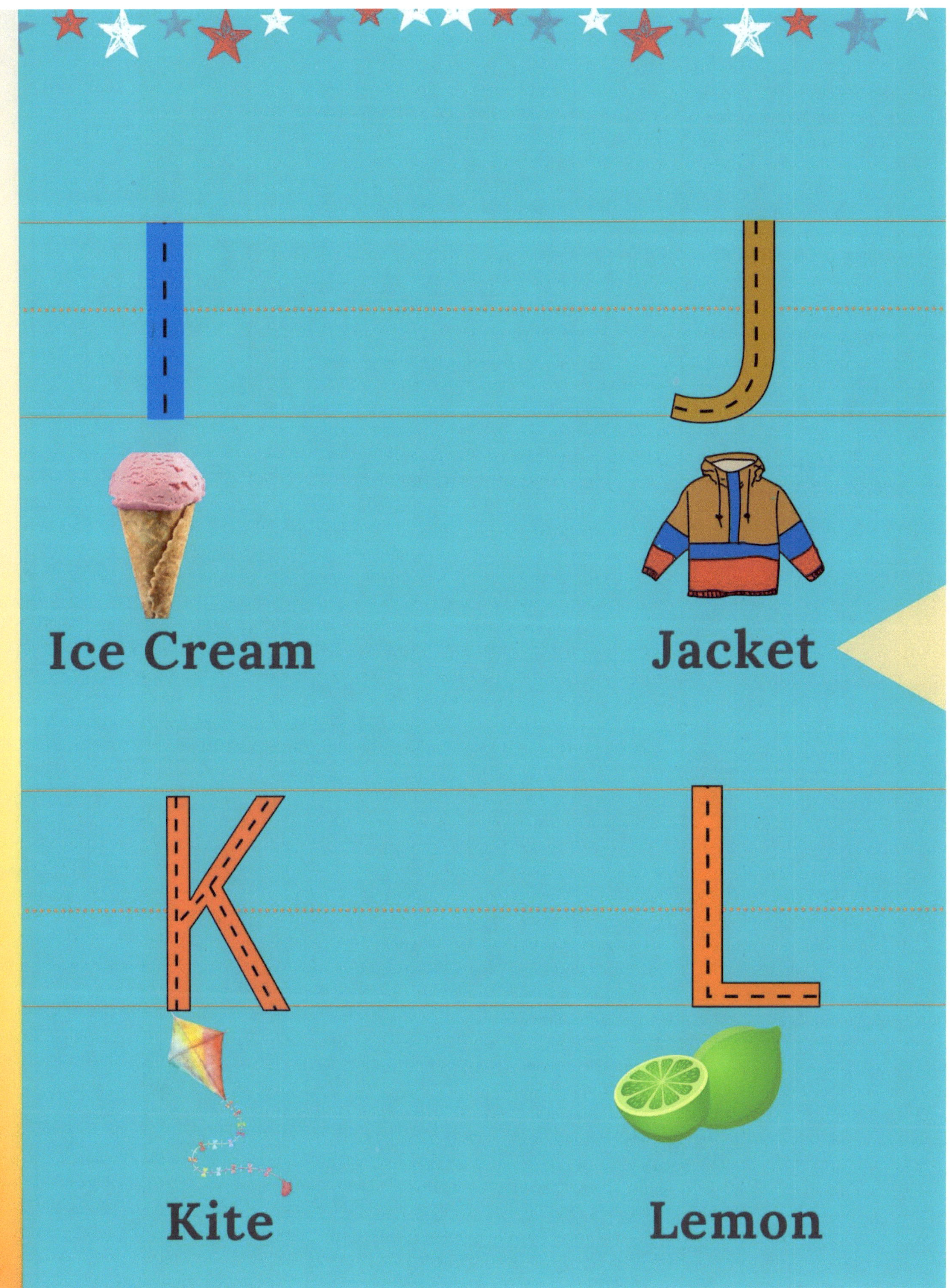

Ice Cream
Jacket
Kite
Lemon

M

Moon

N

Nespaper

O

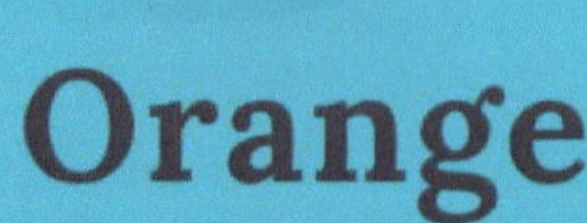

Orange

P

Pen

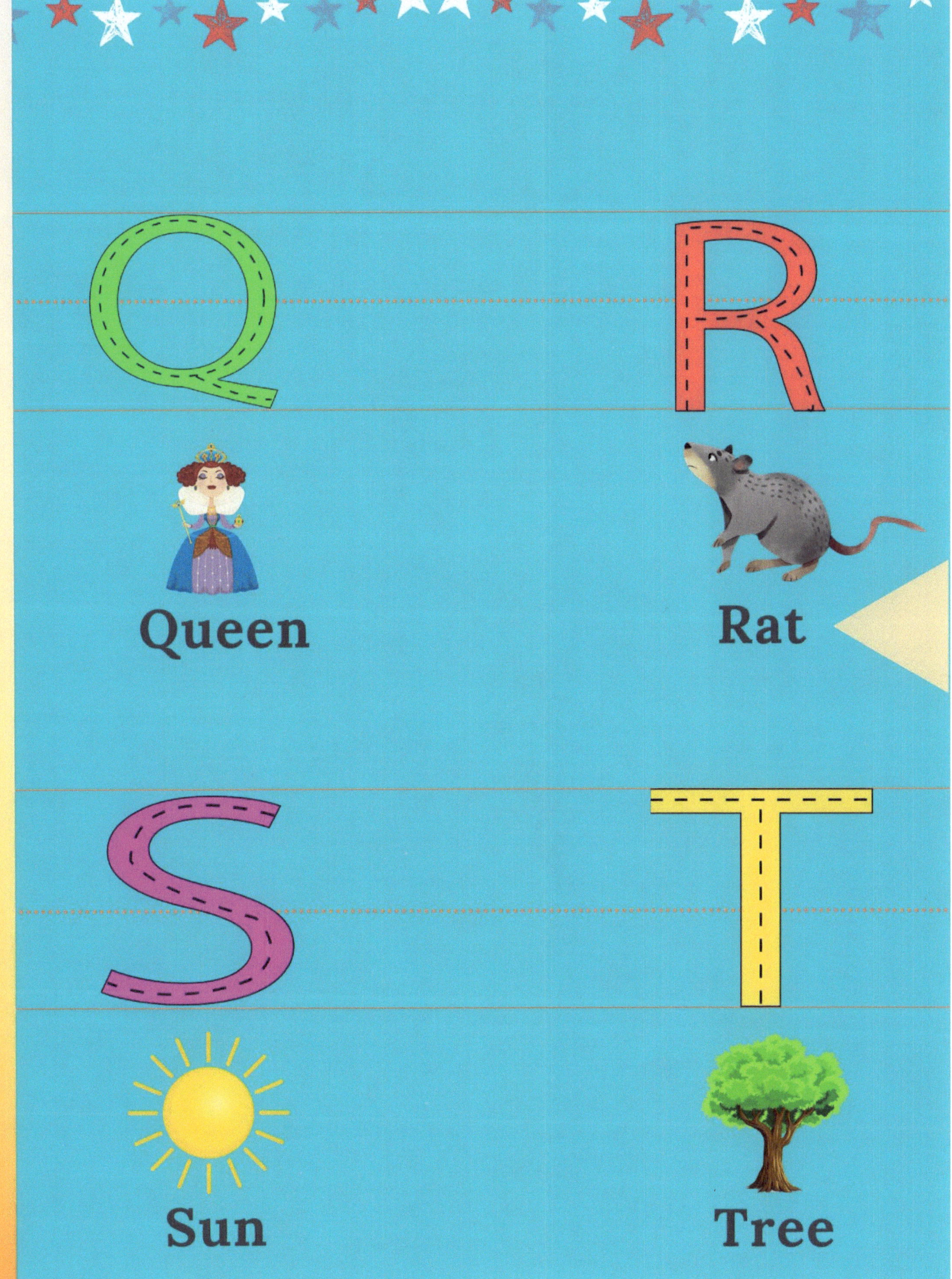

Q

R

Queen

Rat

S

T

Sun

Tree

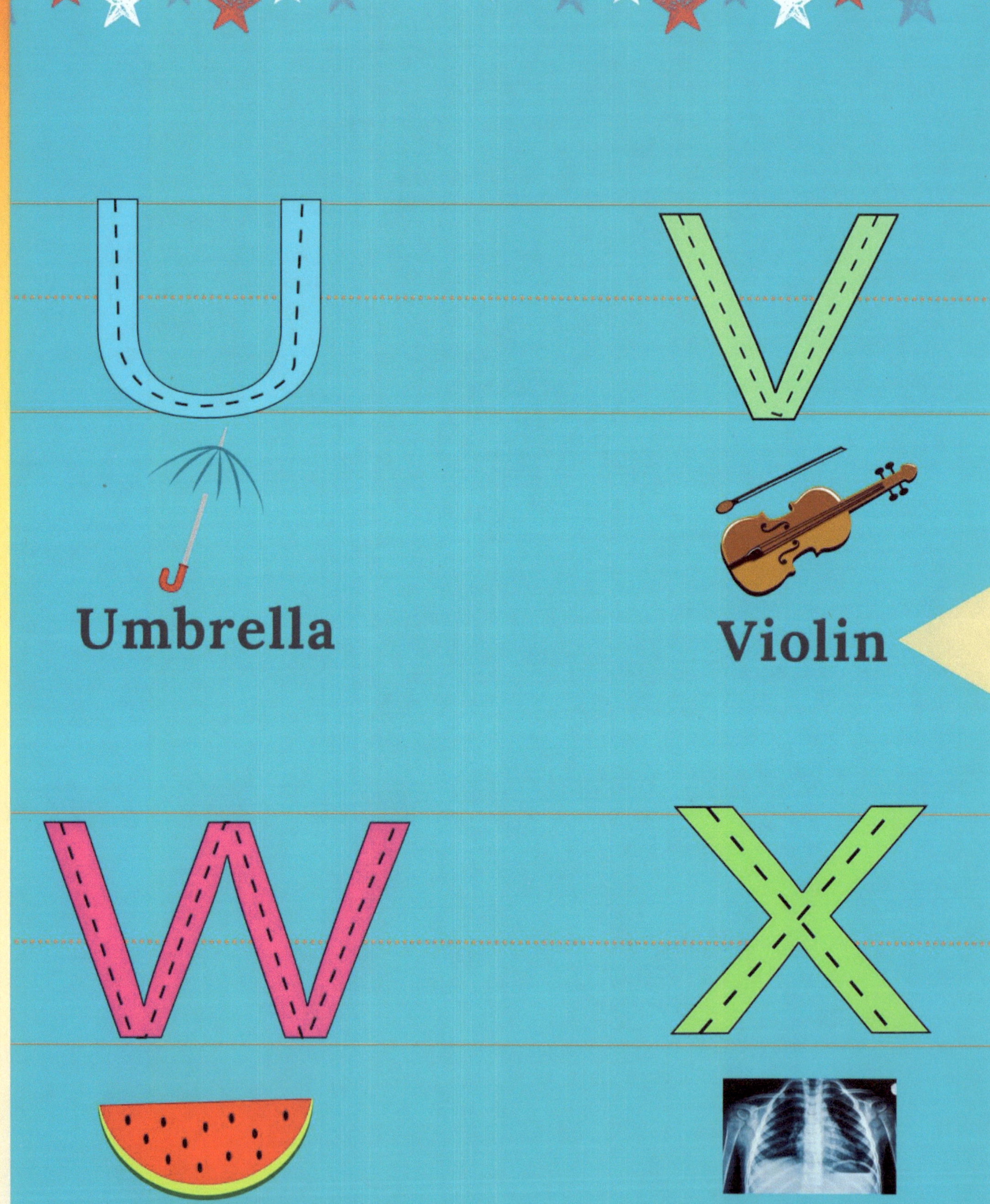

Umbrella

Violin

Watermelon

X-ray

Yo-Yo
Zebra

In Small Letters

a

b

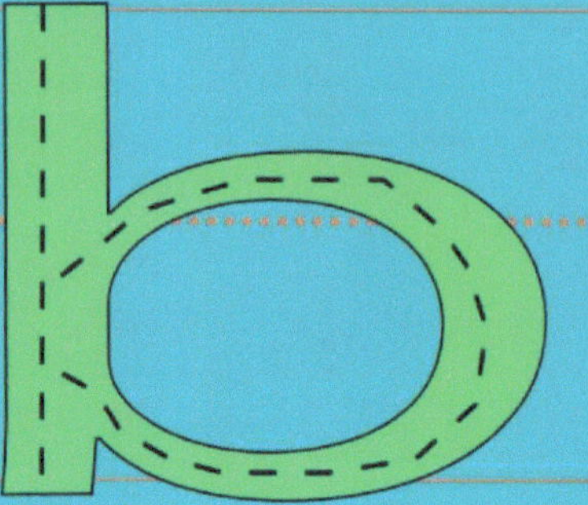

Apple

Ball

c

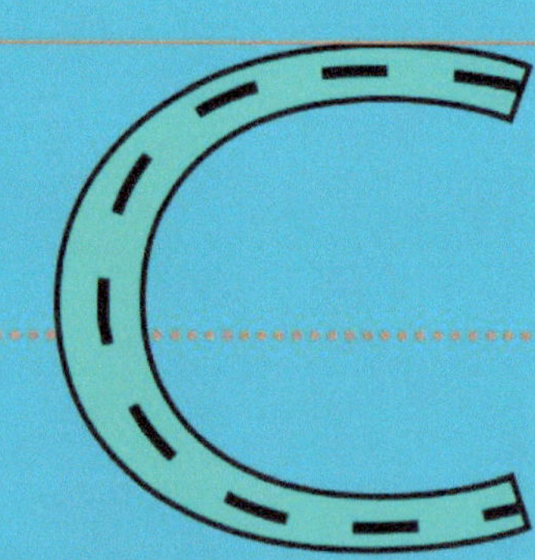

d

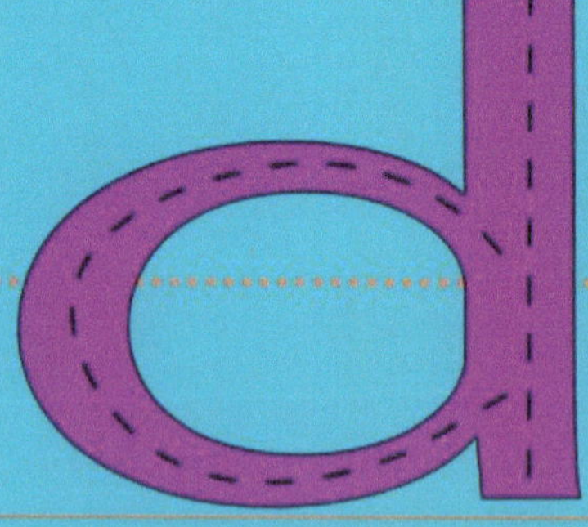

Cat

Dog

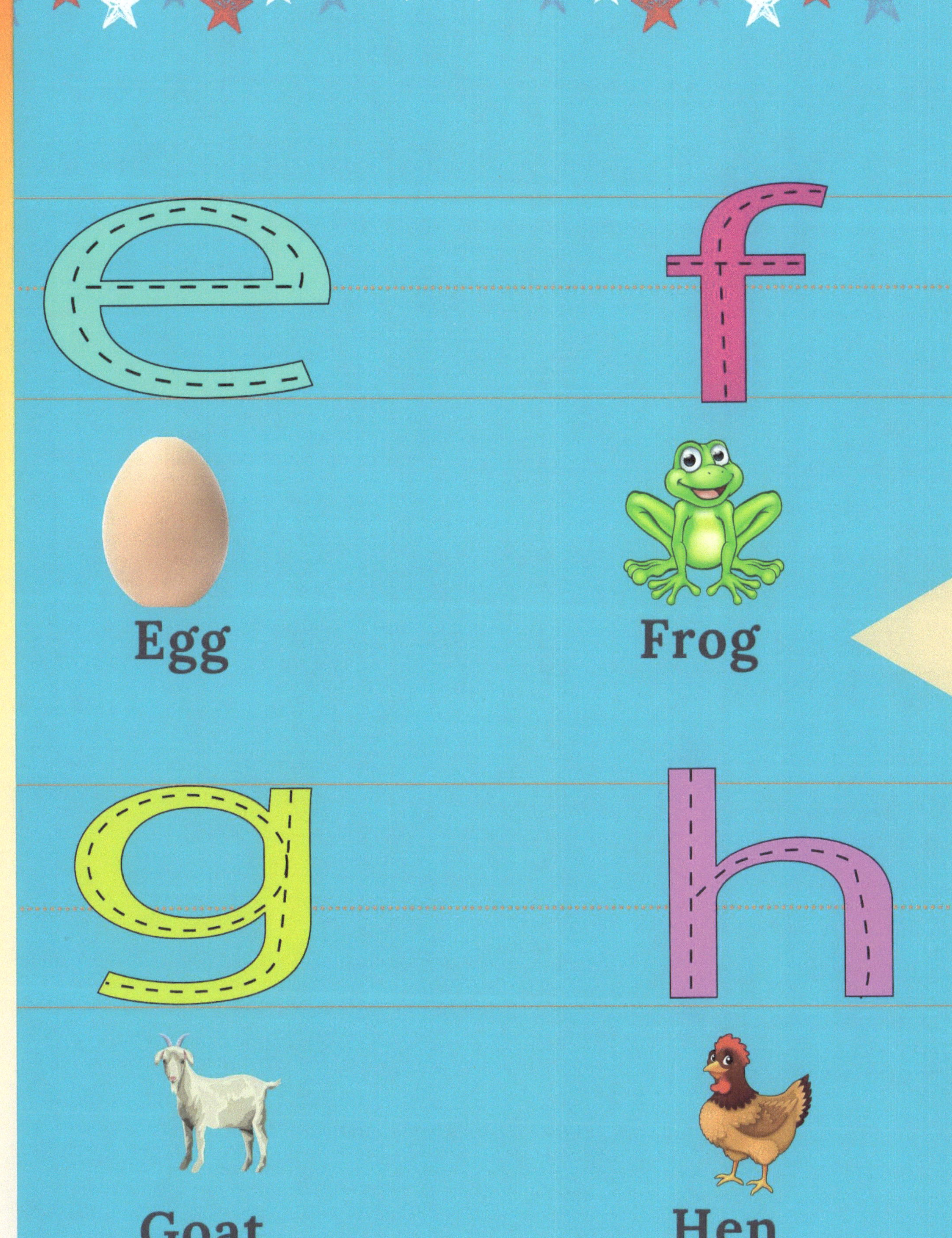

e
f
Egg
Frog
g
h
Goat
Hen

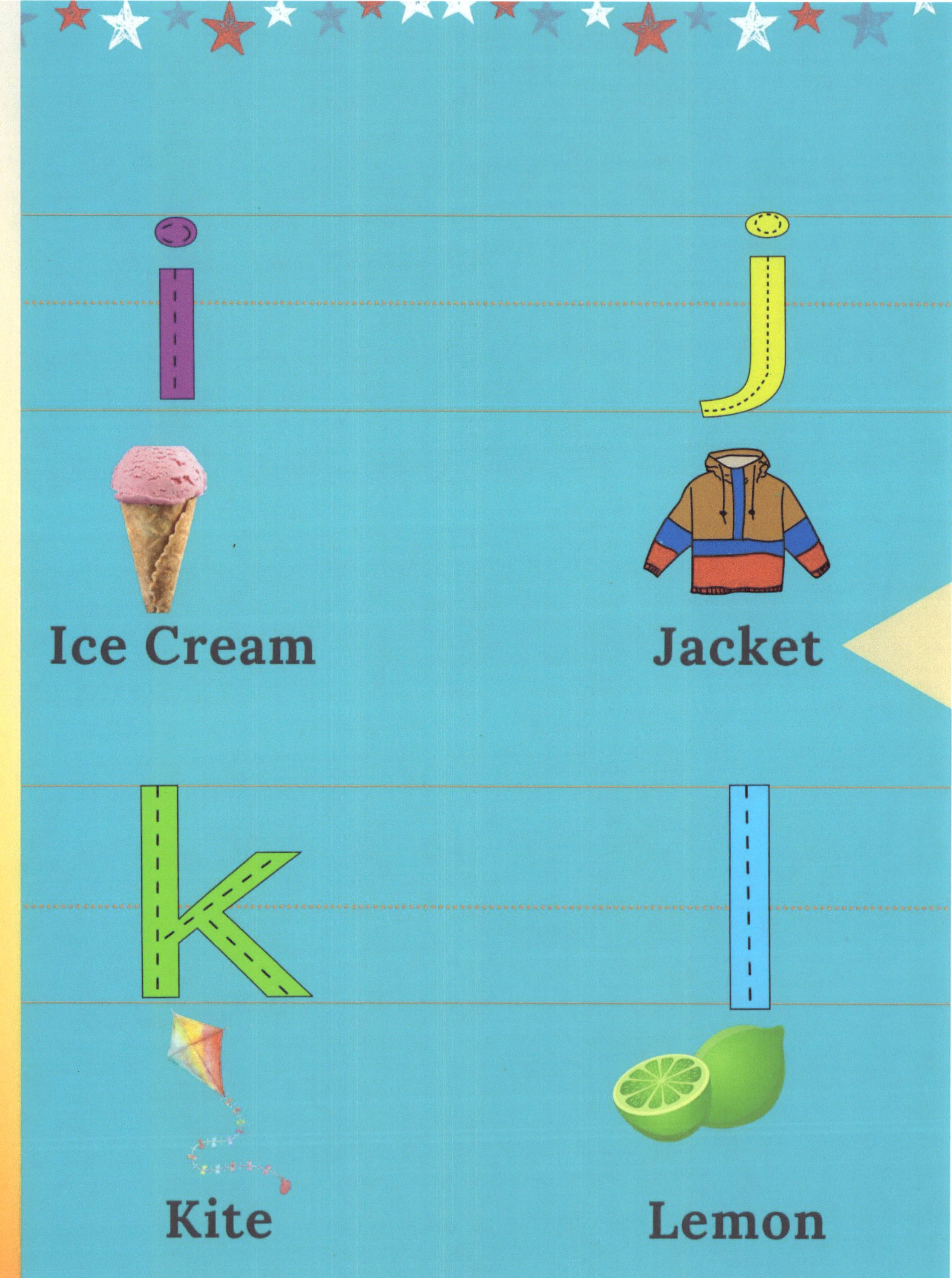

i
j
Ice Cream
Jacket
k
l
Kite
Lemon

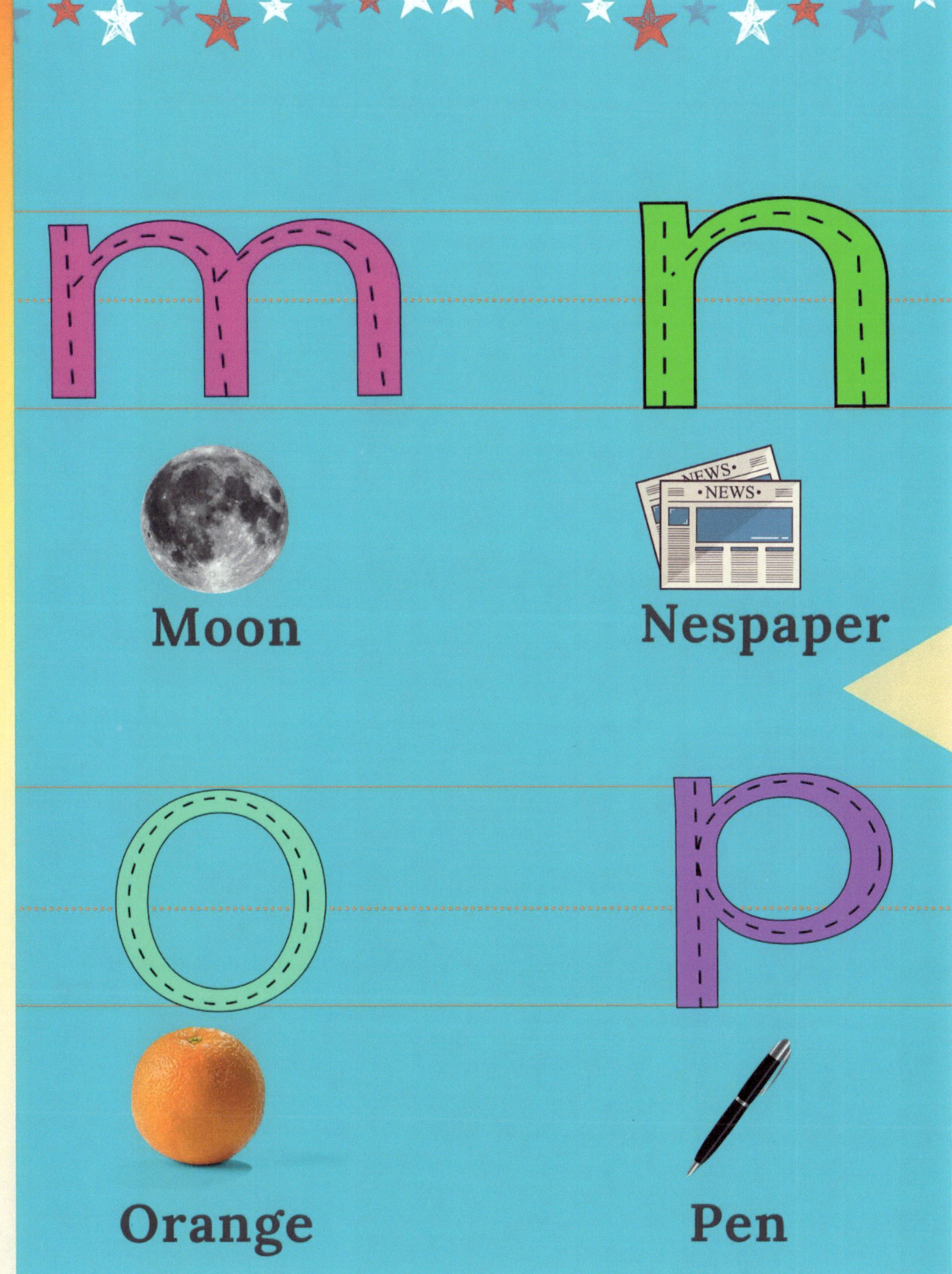

m
n
Moon
Nespaper
o
p
Orange
Pen

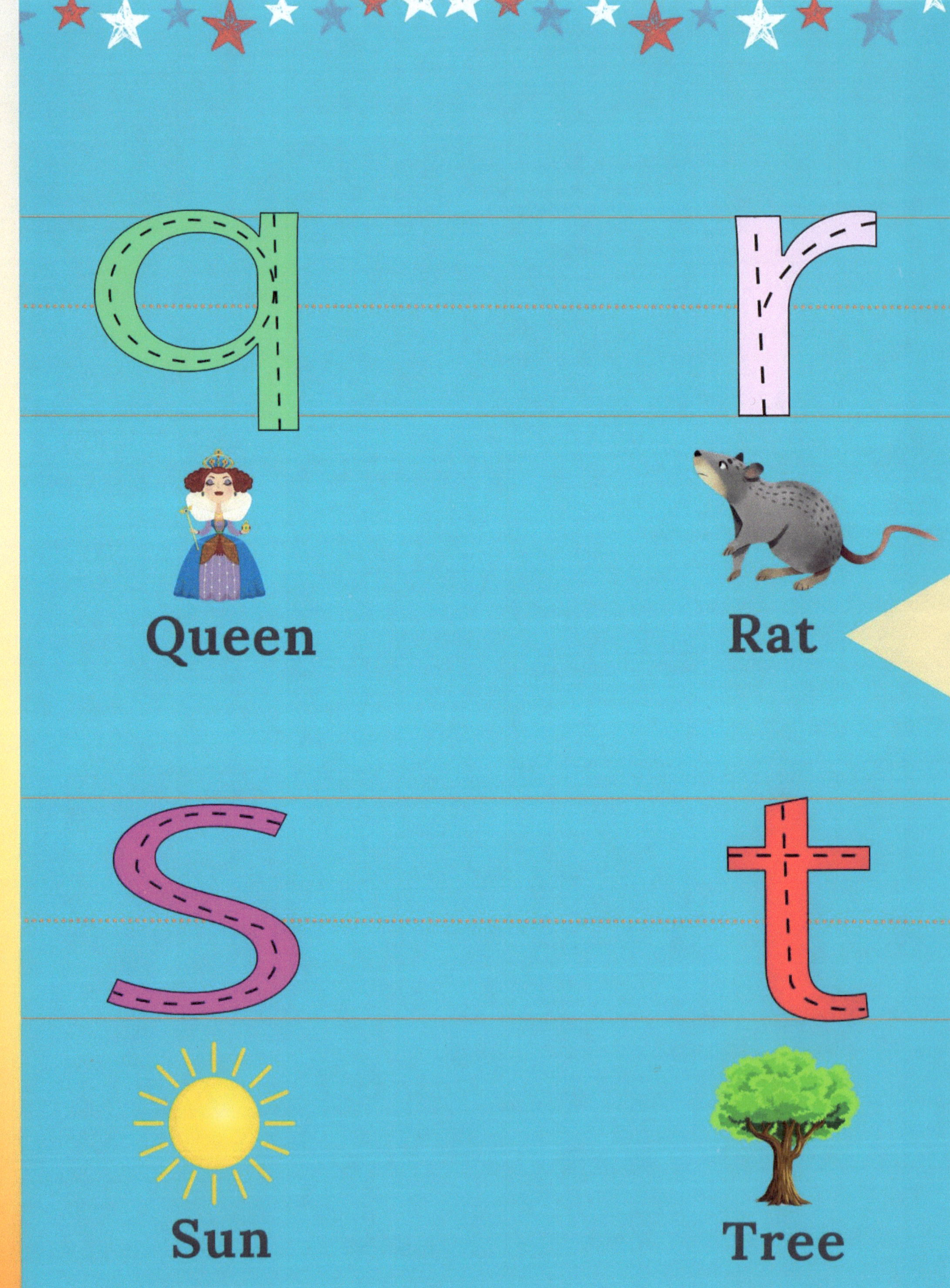

q

r

Queen

Rat

s

t

Sun

Tree

U

Umbrella

V

Violin

W

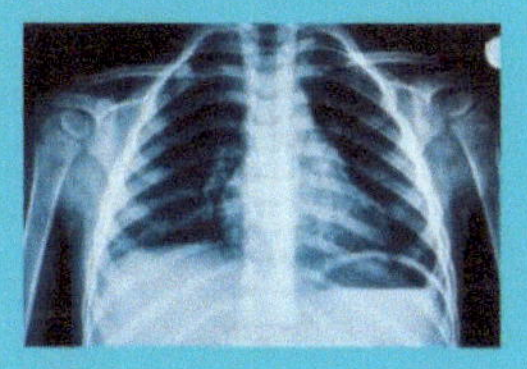

Watermelon

X

X-ray

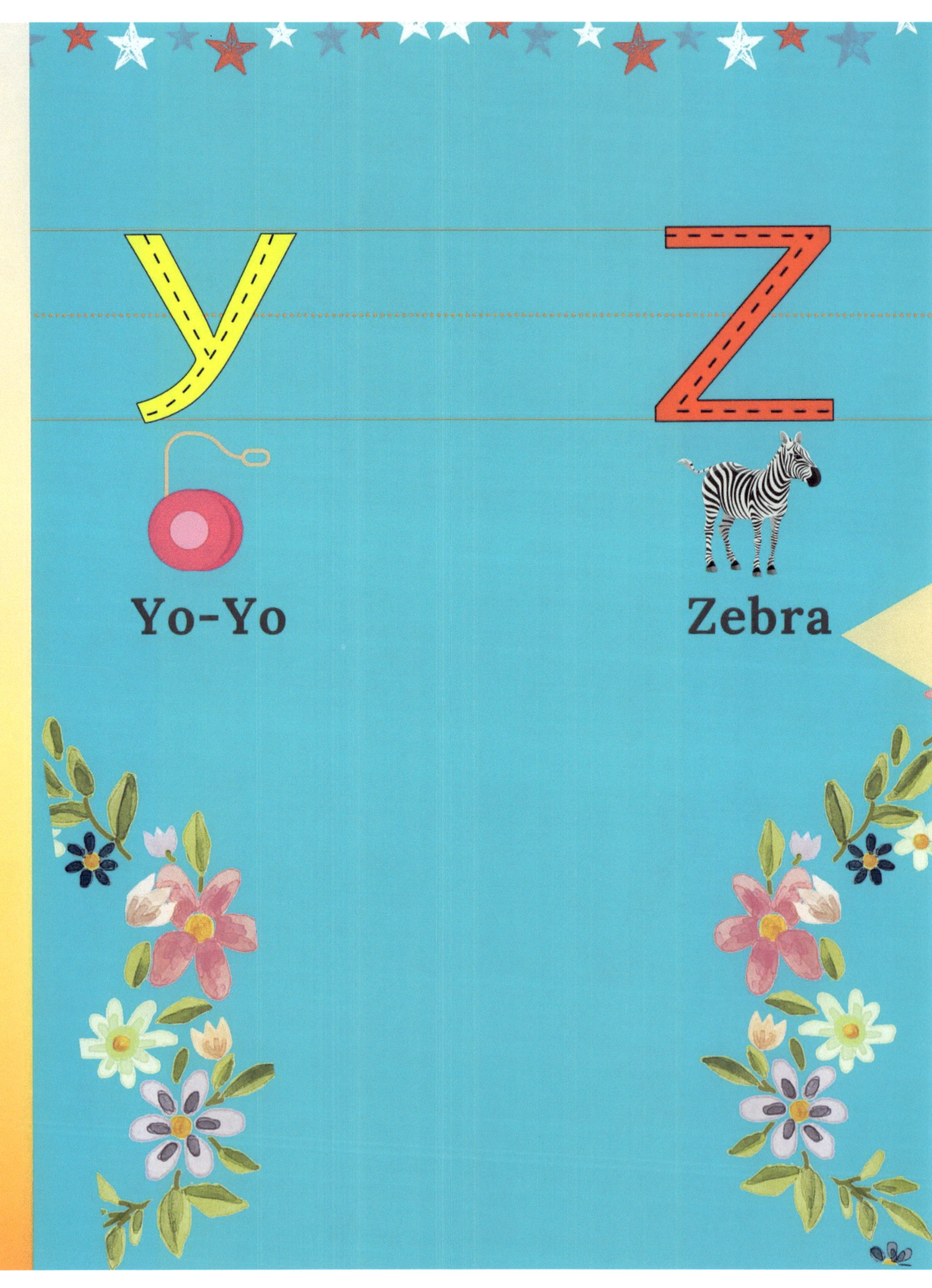

y

Yo-Yo

z

Zebra

Congratulations!!

You have finished A-Z.
You have also finished a-z.

But, You know kid,
Wise sayings
Practice makes a man perfect.

So, Start practicing more
from the next page.

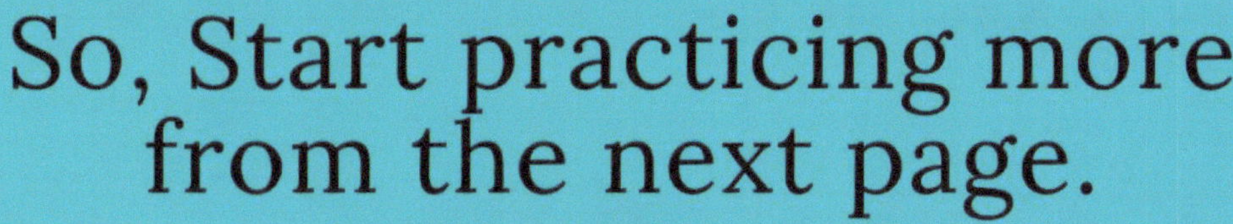

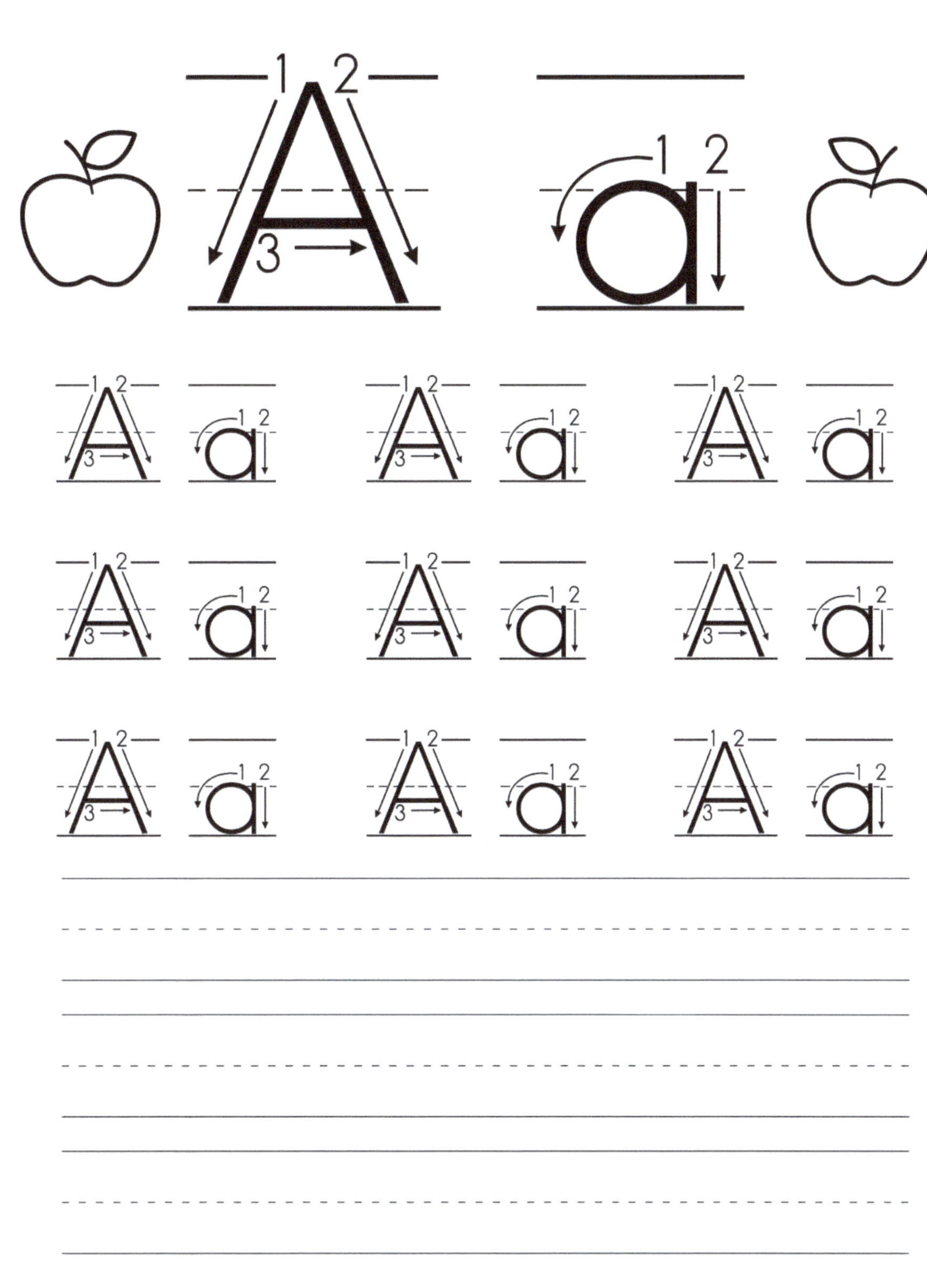

B b
Bb Bb Bb Bb Bb
Bb Bb Bb Bb Bb
Bb Bb Bb Bb Bb

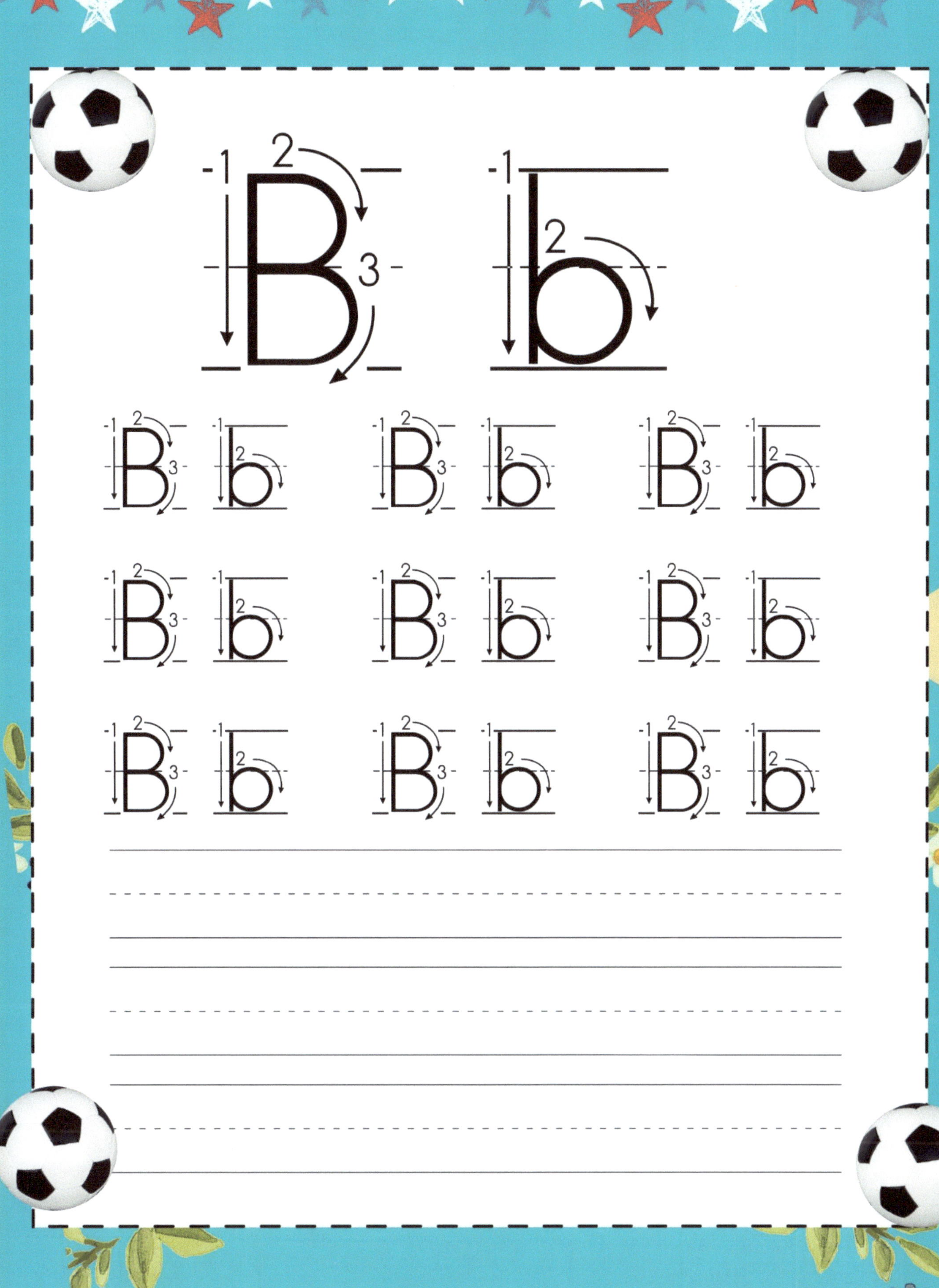

1
1
Cc Cc Cc Cc Cc
Cc Cc Cc Cc Cc
Cc Cc Cc Cc Cc

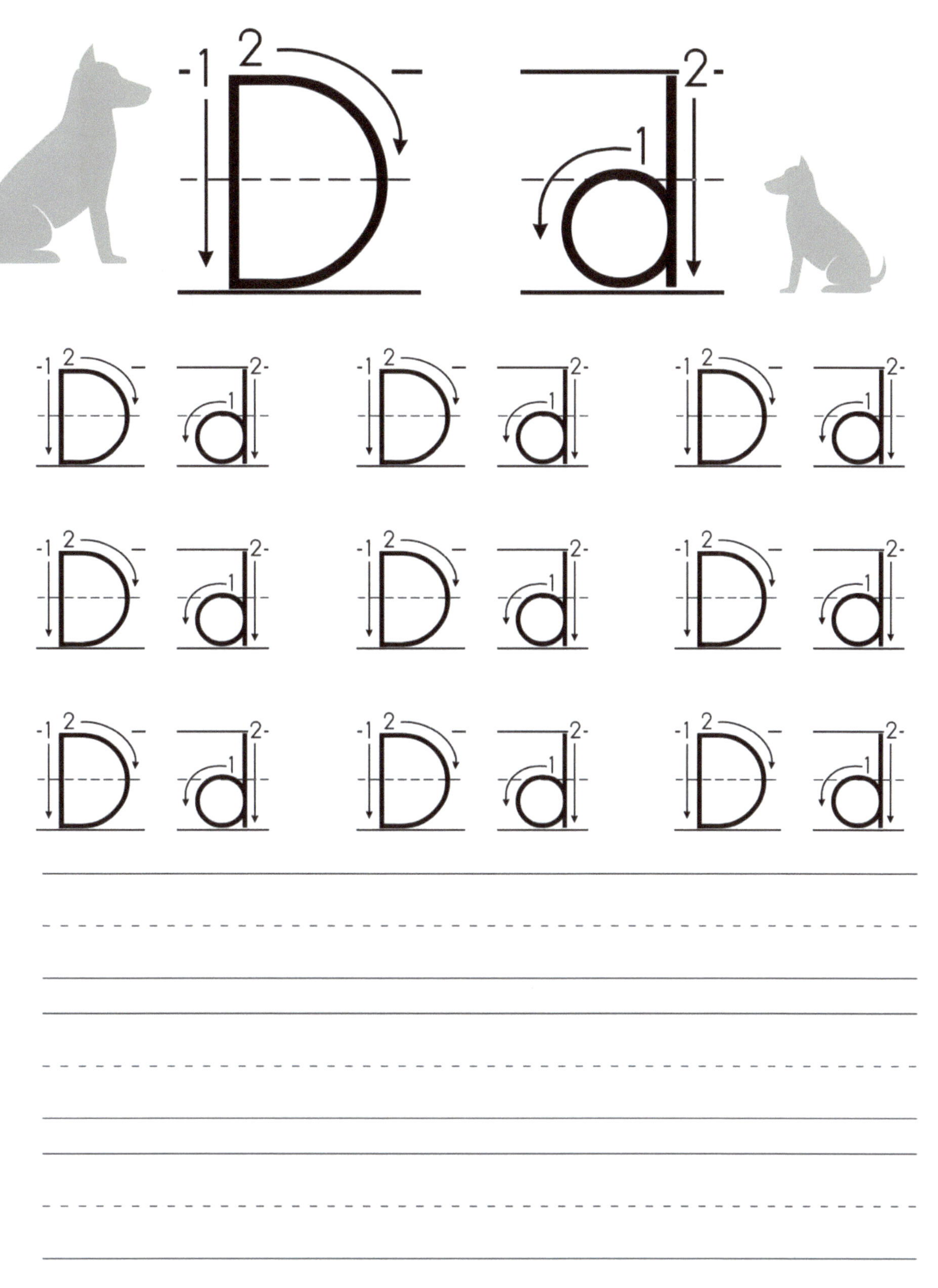

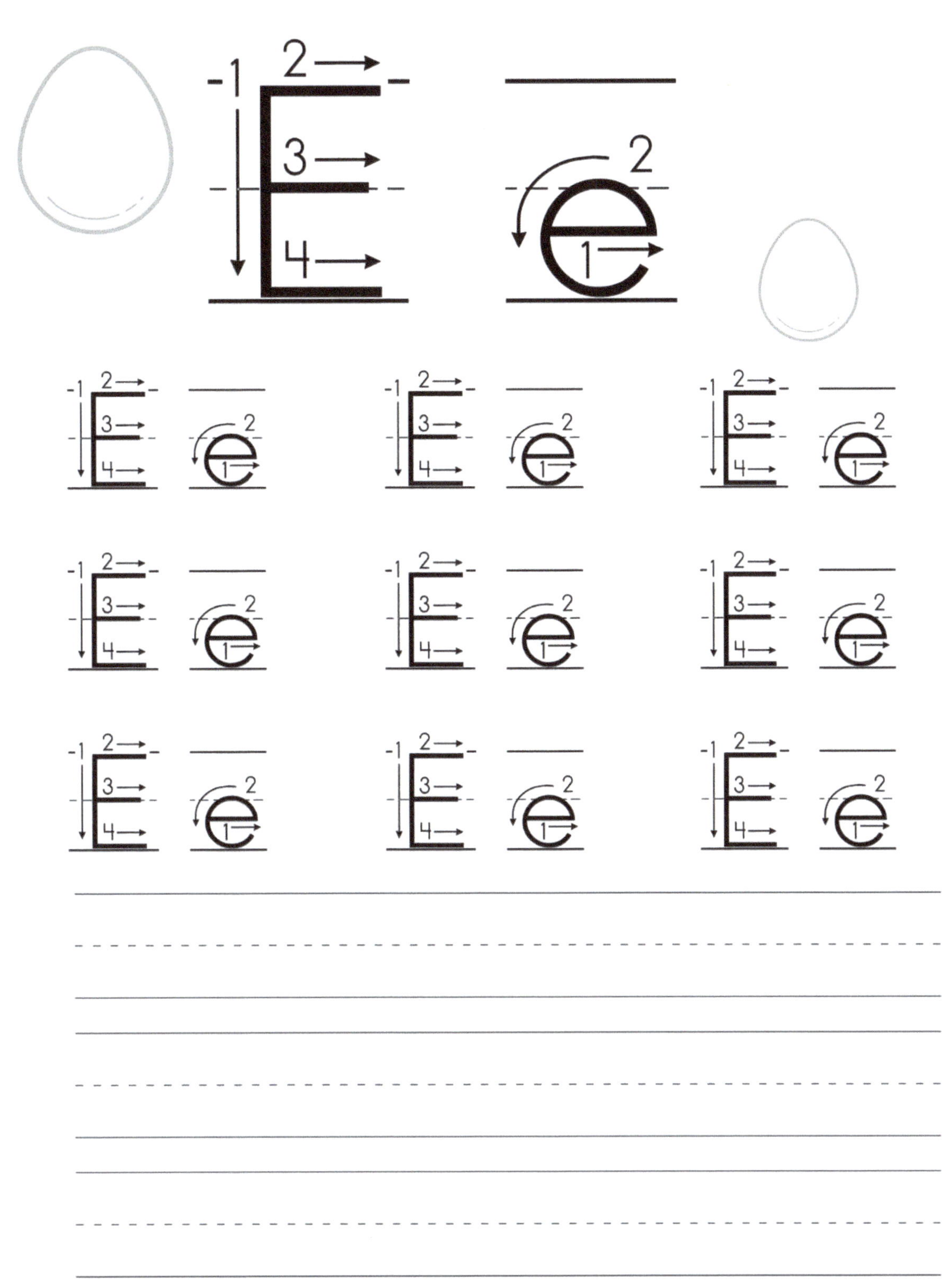

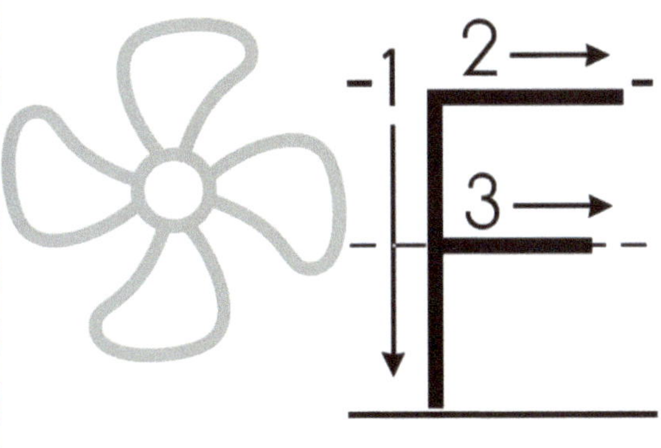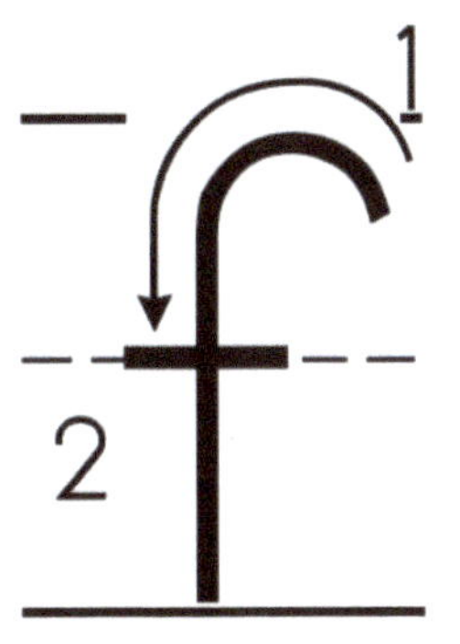

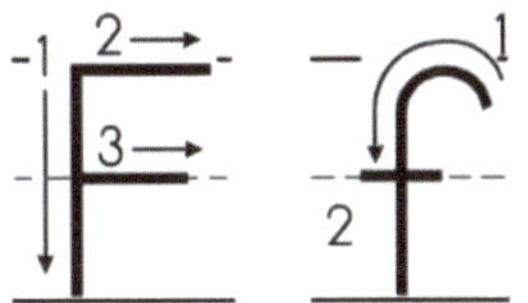

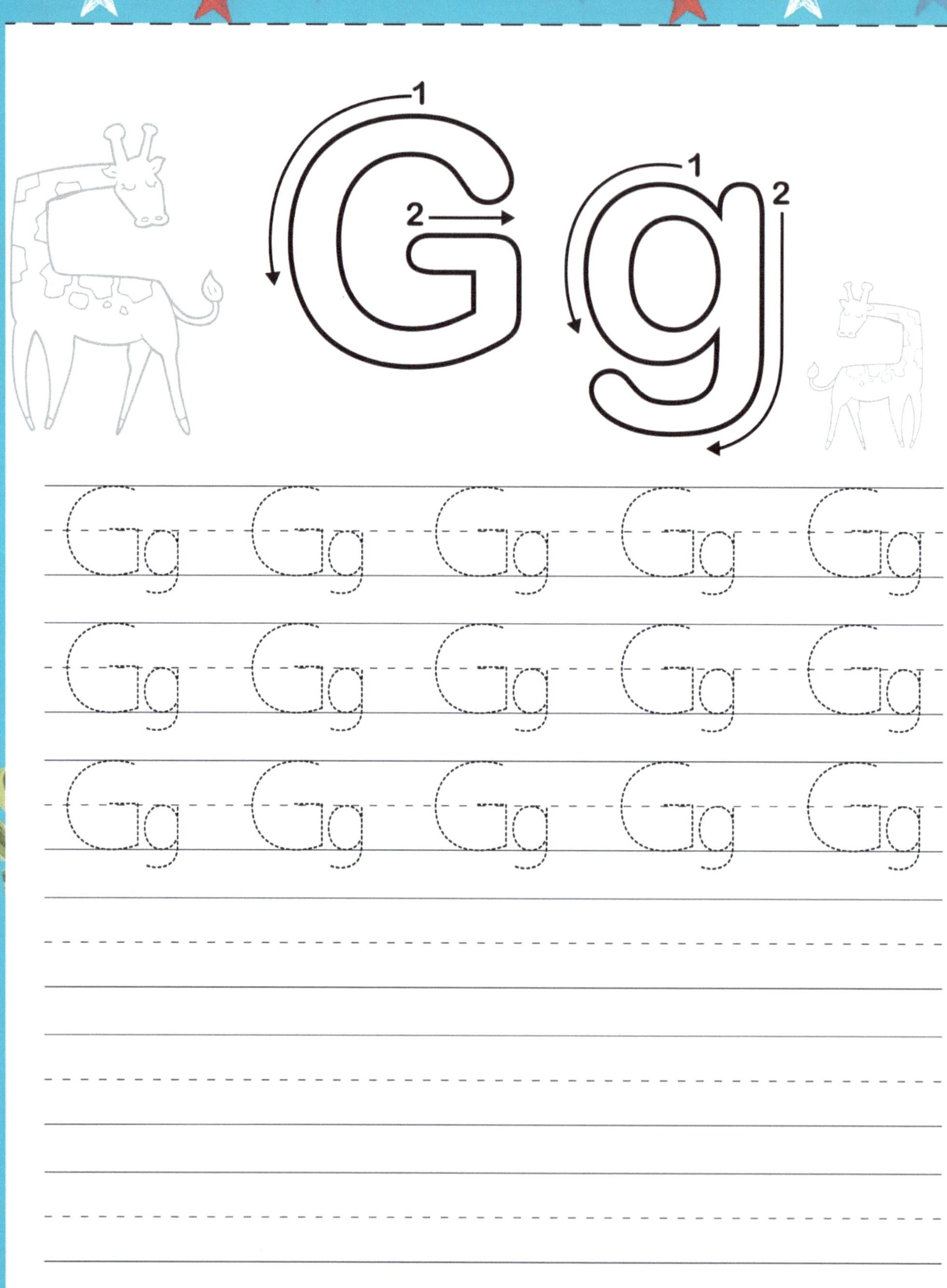

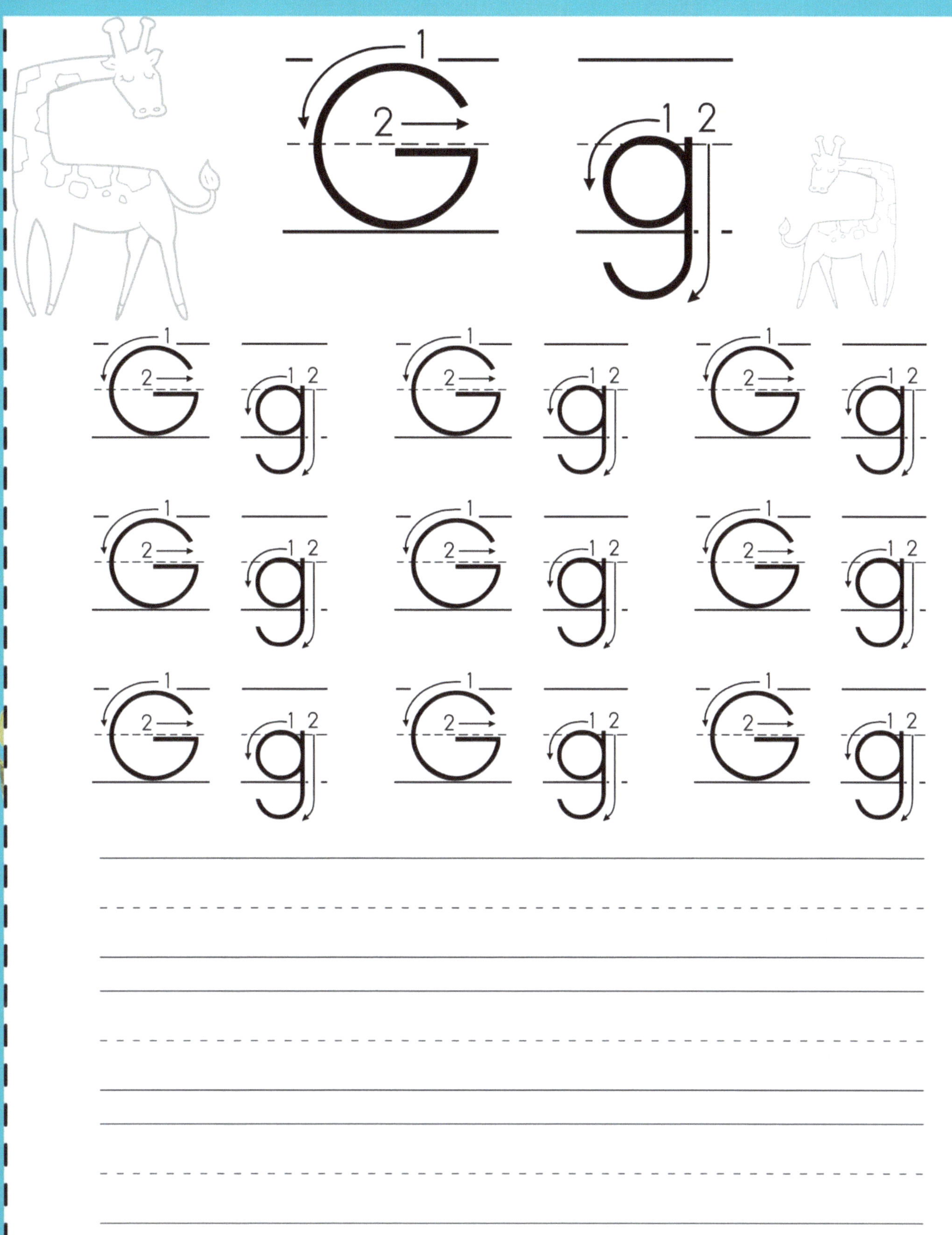

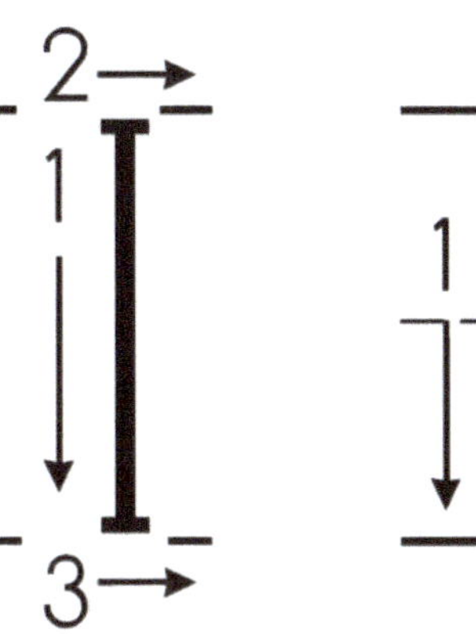

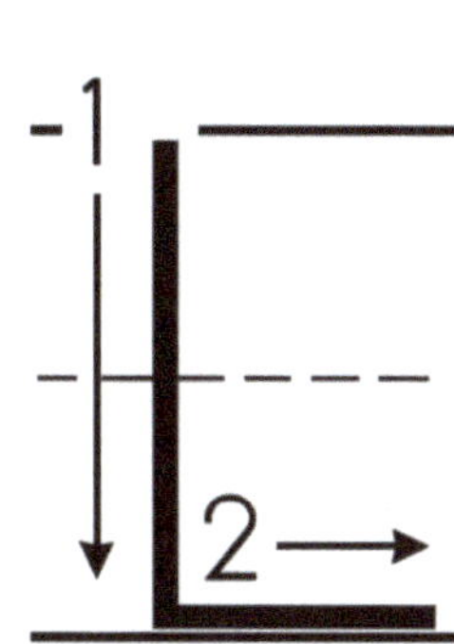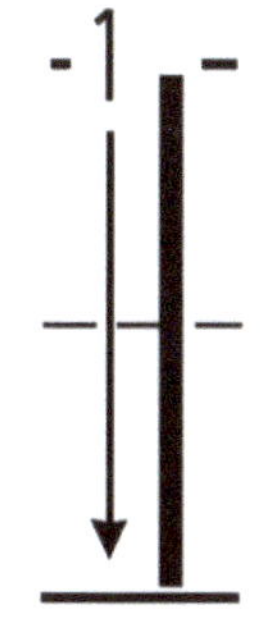

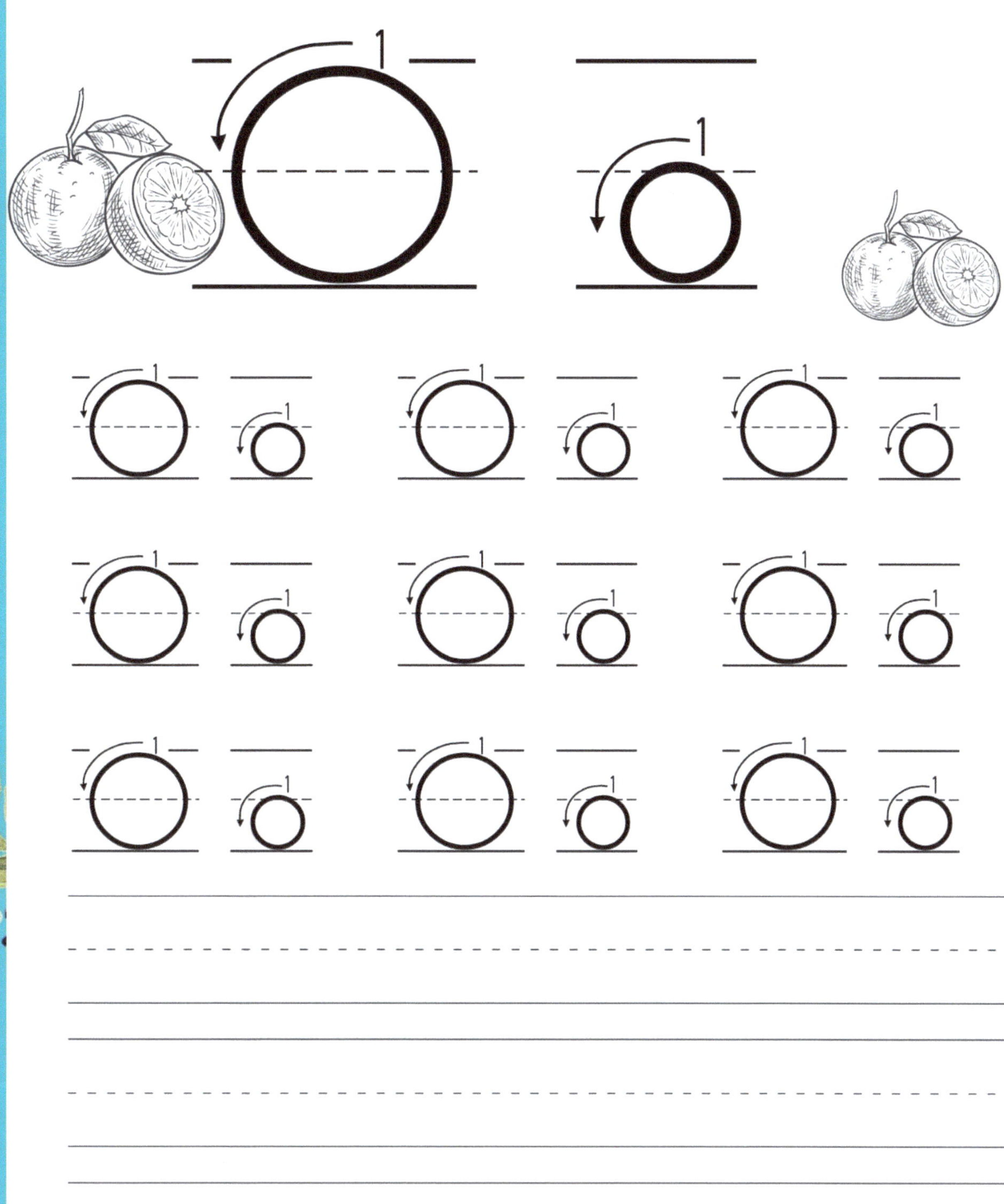

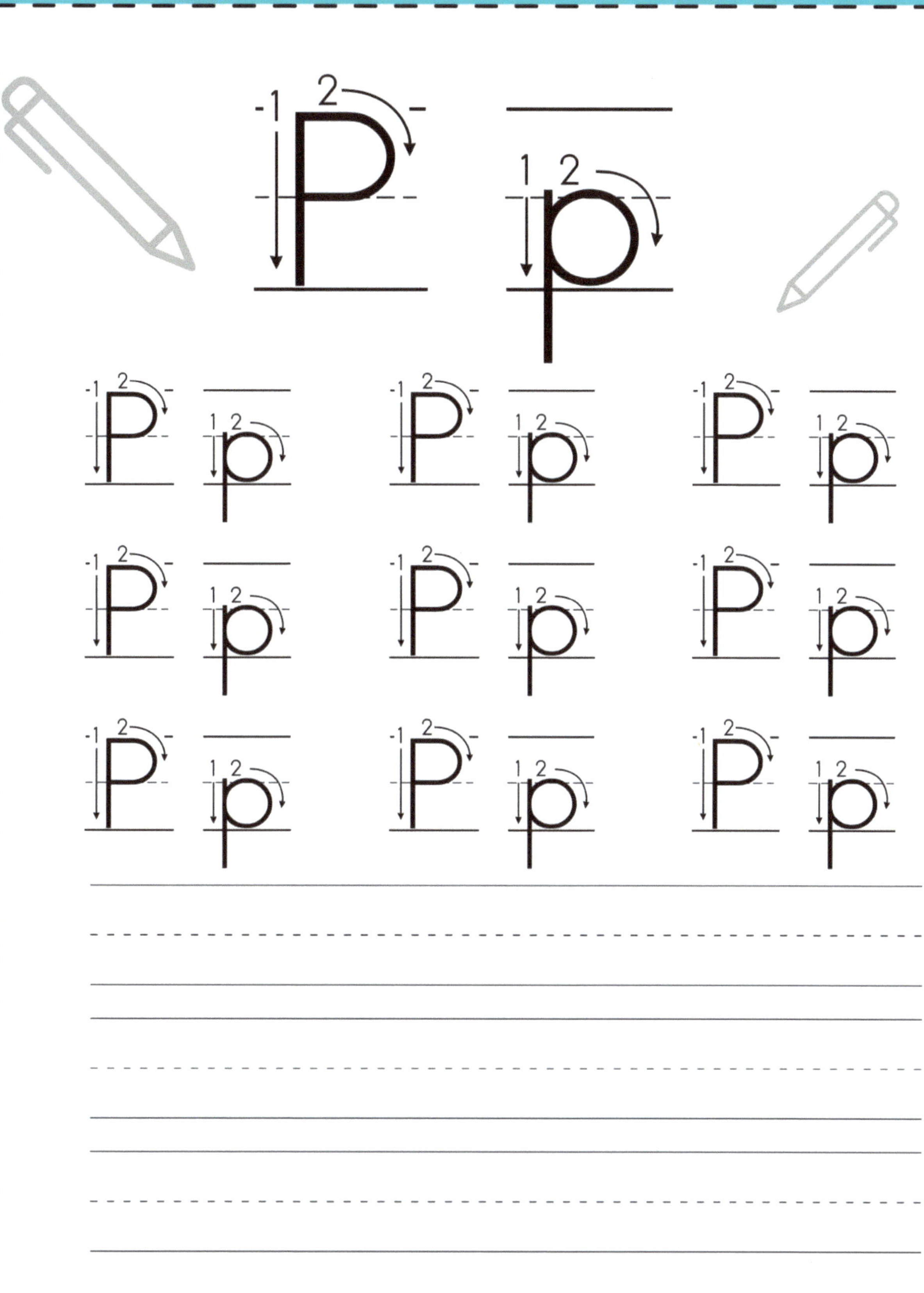

S s

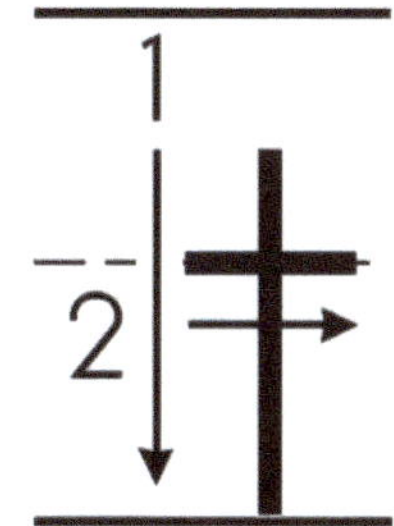

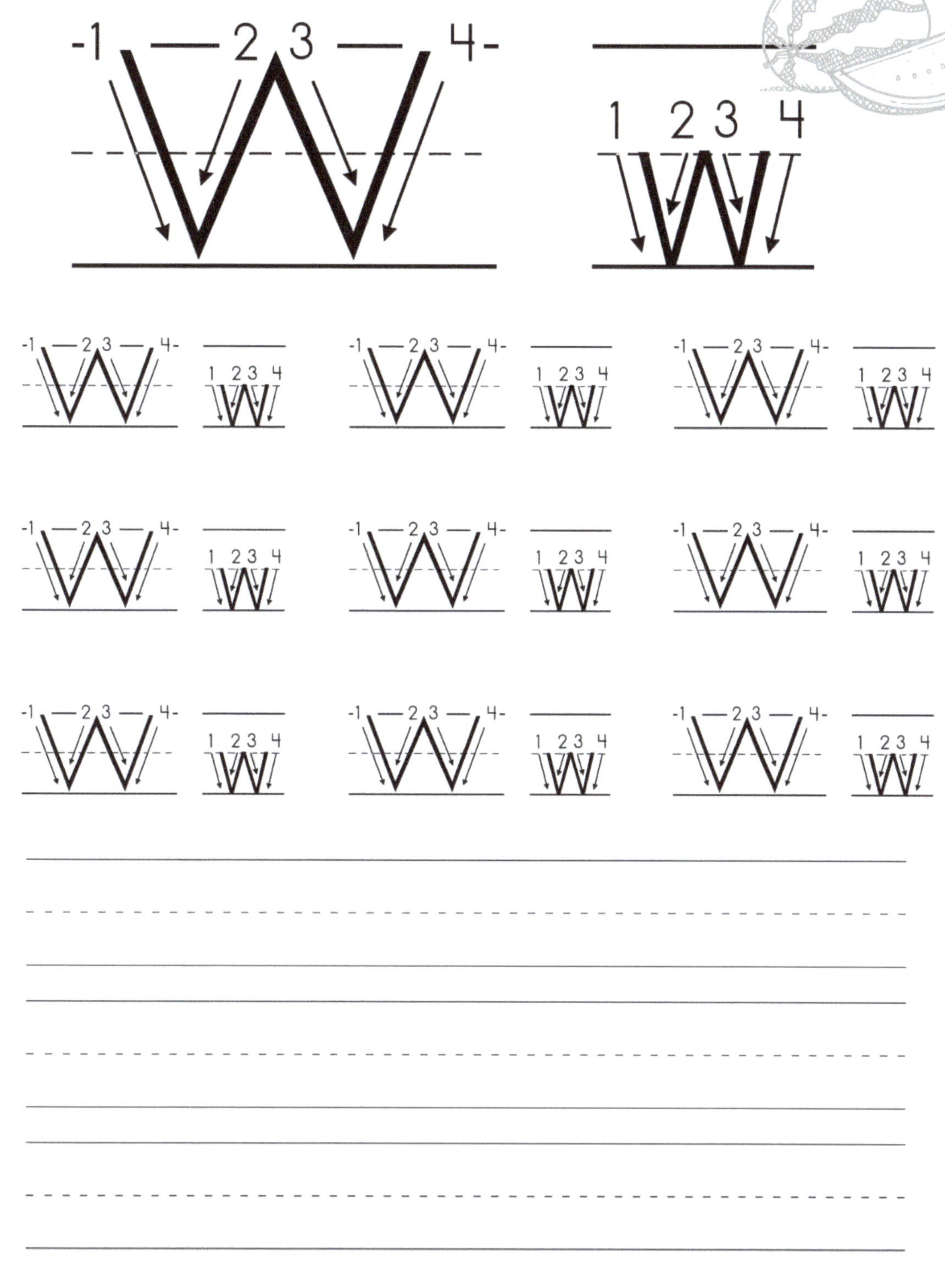

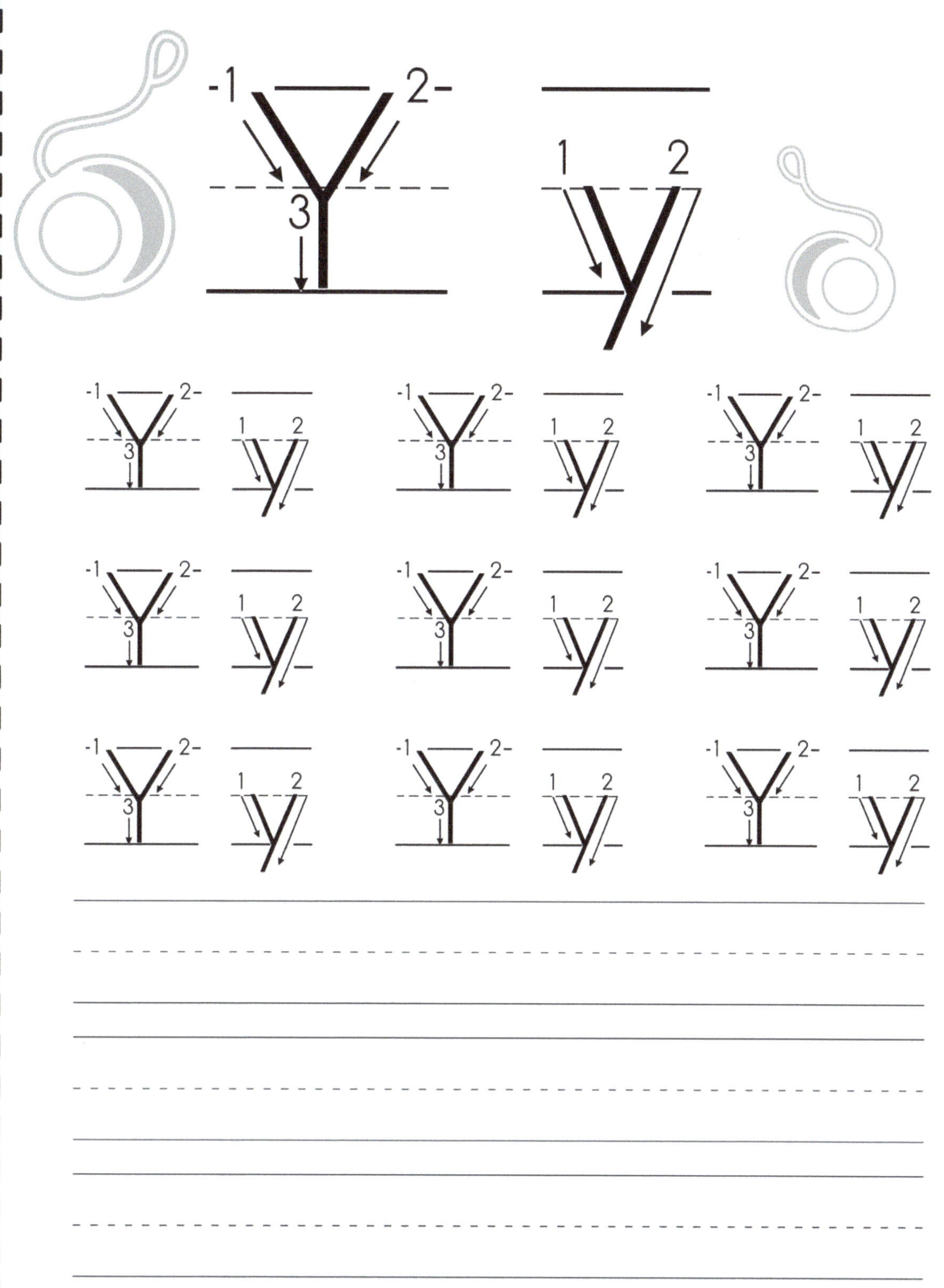

Trace The Numbers

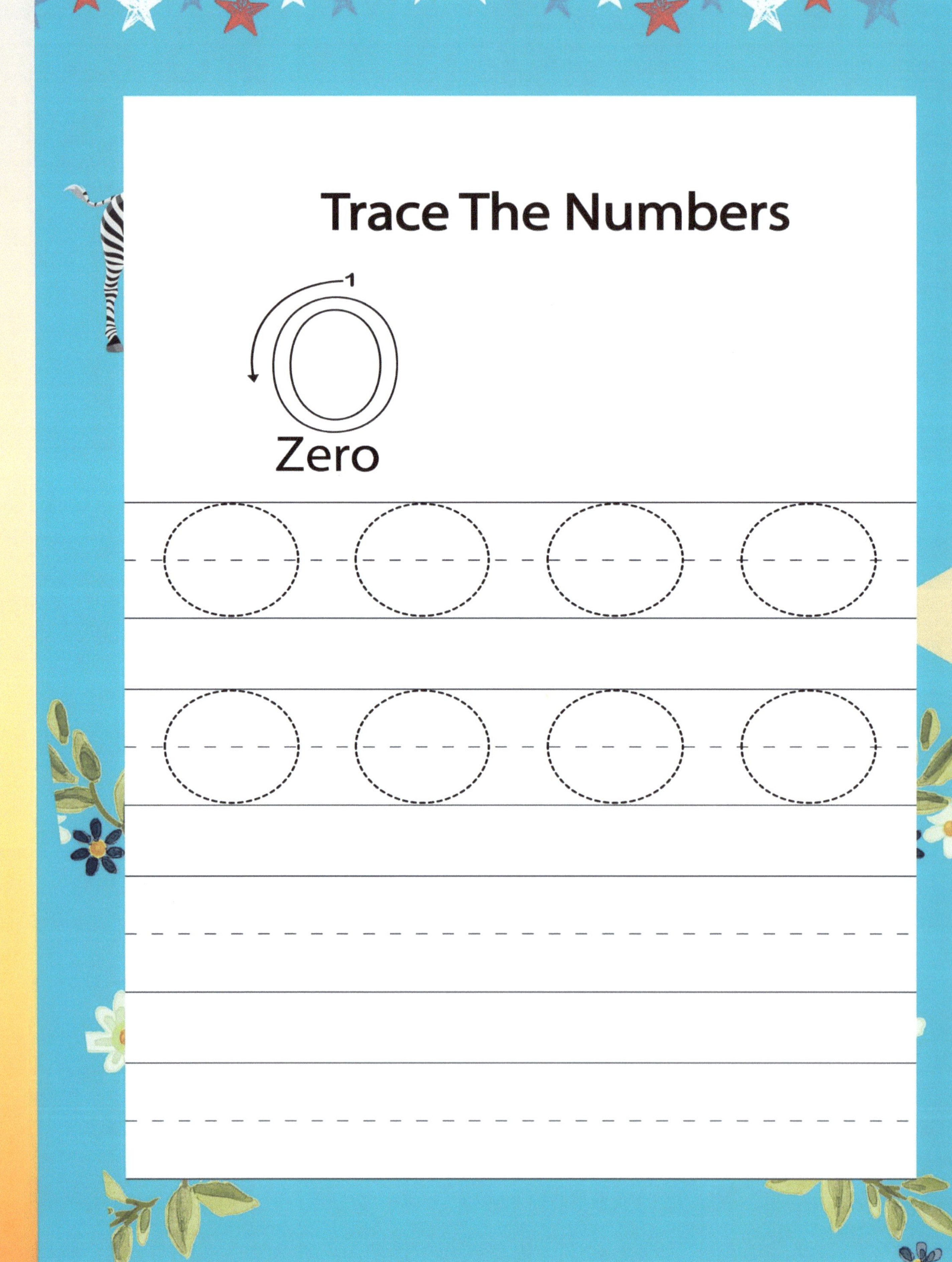

1
2
One

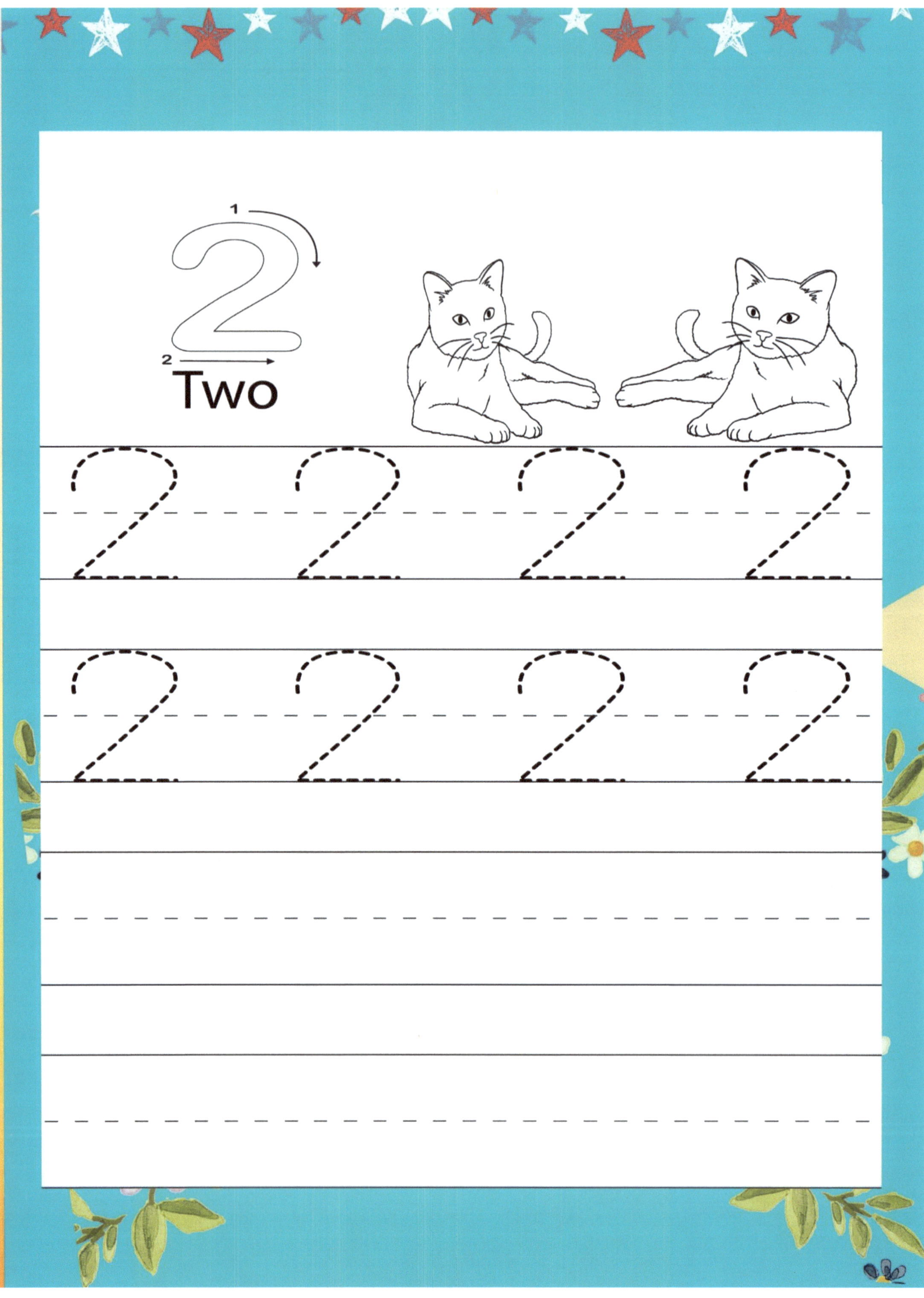

1
2
2
Two

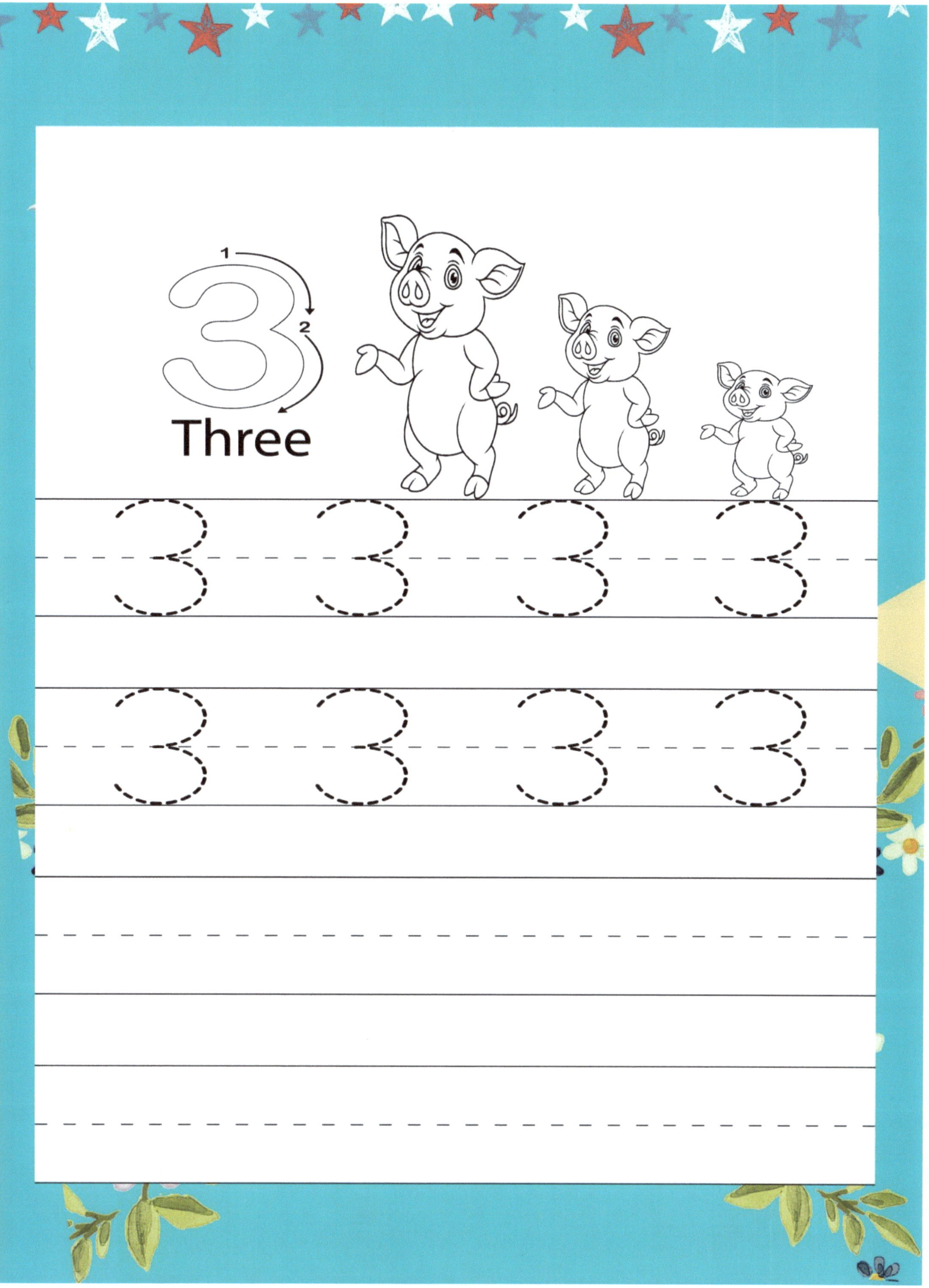

1
2
3
Three
3 3 3 3
3 3 3 3

4

Four

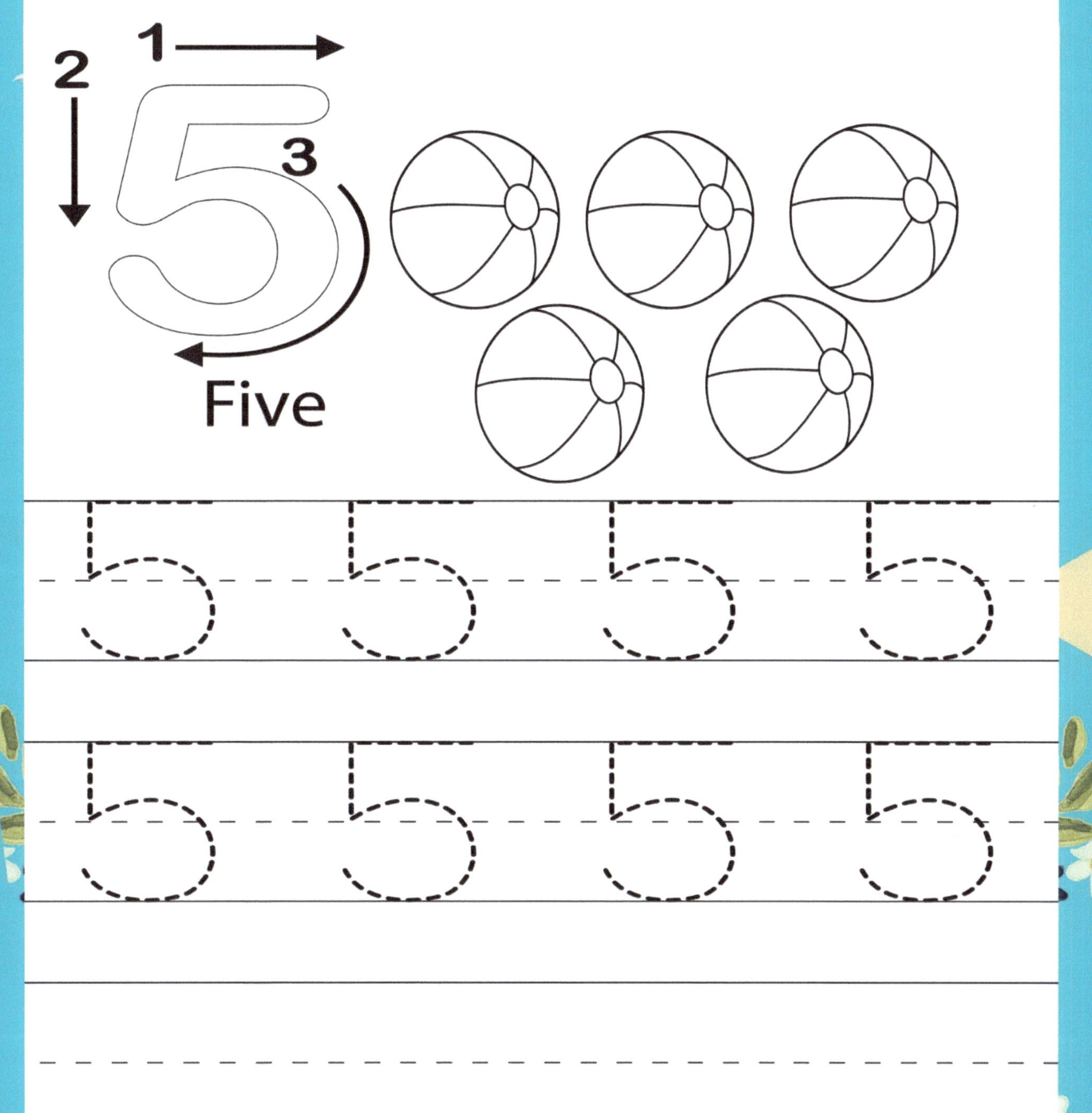

1
2
3
5
Five

1
2
Six
6 6 6 6
6 6 6 6

1
2
Seven

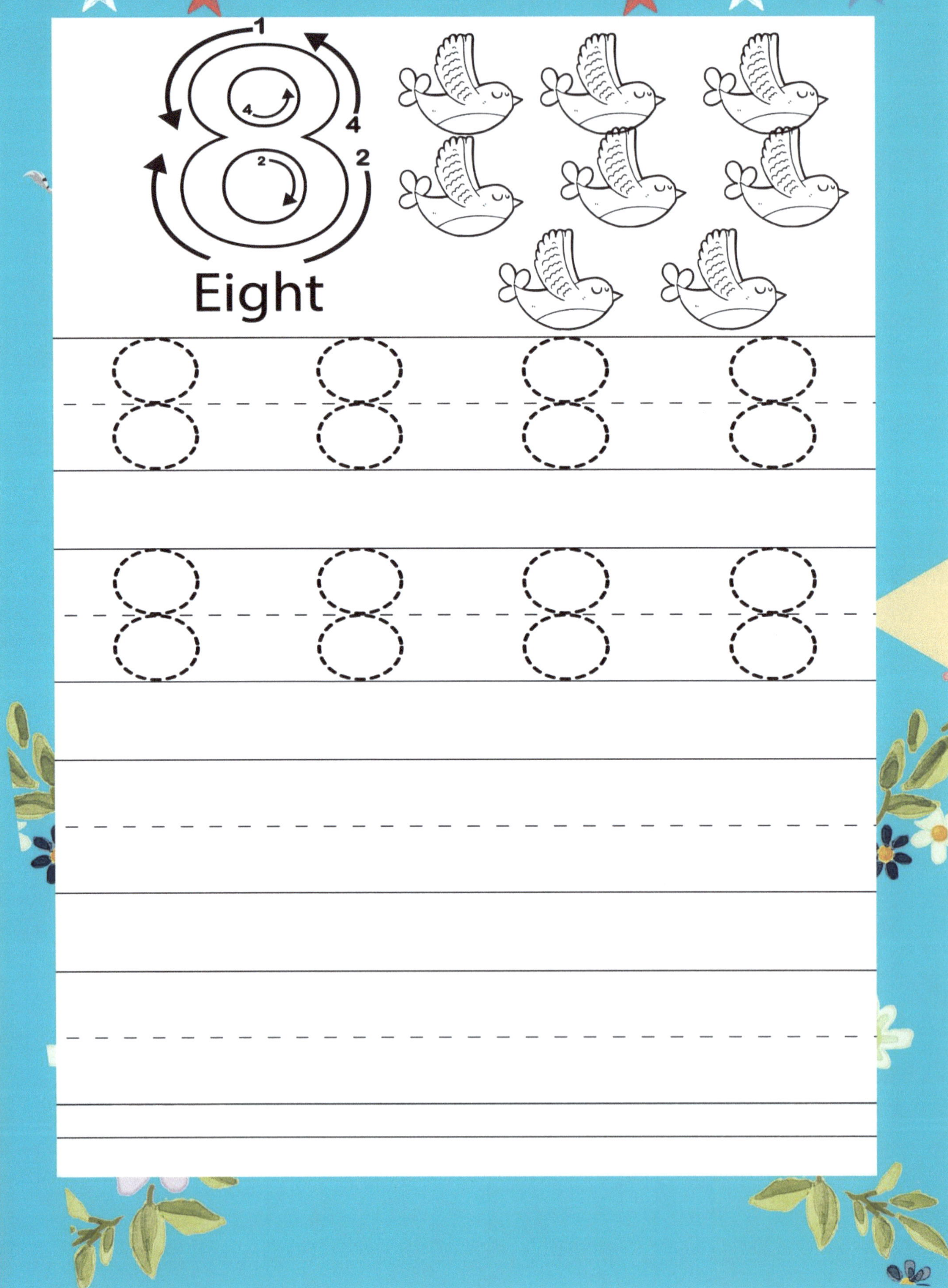

1
4
4
2
2
Eight

9
Nine

BEST OF LUCK FOR YOUR FUTURE